Hello,
Fruit Face!

The Paintings of
Giuseppe Arcimboldo

Prestel Adventures in Art

Spring is showing off her new clothes

You can almost smell this messenger of spring, made largely of flowers and leaves. Our eyes automatically turn the delicate roses into a cheek, a chin or red lips—and this is just what the artist wanted at the time he painted them.

It's pure magic. Sit back and marvel at this mysterious master, who creates human features from flowers: a peony becomes an ear, and the dangling honeysuckle makes a lovely earring. A closed lily forms a nose, while the hair is a sea of different flowers—hibiscus, mallow and pomegranate blossoms. An opened lily shoots boldly out of the fine head of plaited hair. Or is this supposed to be a bonnet to match the dress of leaves, grass and herbs, with its fashionably gathered cabbage-leaf shoulders and its high collar of white forget-me-nots and small daisies? No matter how we piece this puzzle together, we will always see the messenger of spring in front of us. In her warm and gentle manner, she cheerfully announces the awakening of Nature.

Spring seems to be smiling at someone opposite. Who could that be, we wonder?

She is not alone, for the artist painted the other seasons as well. Let's take a closer look . . .

Spring is the first,
Then Summer and Fall
Cold Winter the last:
Four seasons in all

Summer is surrounded by the fruits of her work

Cherries, plums, berries, pears, melons, corn, and barley.

But there is certainly much more to discover here.
Take a look at the cucumber which forms Summer's nose,
and the apple making a cheerfully chubby cheek.
Garlic cloves and a cob of corn rub noses with an egg plant
and pieces of fruit, with a mass of grapes
and a plump melon forming a wild head of hair.
The cherry eye glistens, while the mouth reveals
a small row of teeth in the form of an open pea pod.

But who is Summer smiling at, we wonder?

Her jacket is made from a finely woven wickerwork of wheat,
with a stiff, high collar.
Here we can clearly make out the artist's name:
"Giuseppe Arcimboldo·F" — "F" is the abbreviation for the Latin
word "fecit", which means Giuseppe Arcimboldo "made this".
The artist has even woven in the date: 1573.

So, now we know that our magician's name is Giuseppe,
and he lived more than 400 years ago.
Do you think this is how all artists painted back then?

5

Autumn is wearing
a crown of grapes

This robust figure is crowned with vine leaves and grapes that are harvested in the autumn. His head is perched above an old wine barrel, held together with willow shoots. A snail is making its leisurely way across the melon—or rather the head of our autumnal friend! The fruity face is plump and ripe, and the fig that dangles from the mushroom ear has burst open, revealing its succulent, red flesh. A pomegranate — a messenger from the warm south—makes a strong chin, over which a bushy beard grows, and the fruit of the open, prickly chestnut gives Autumn his tongue. He looks as if he is eagerly awaiting a chance to taste all these delicious things!

Autumn promises a rich harvest, doesn't he?

Winter is looking rather gloomy

Well, of course, he must be really cold!

His features peer out from a gnarled tree trunk and, around his roots, virtually all the earth that has been keeping him warm has been washed away. That's enough to put anyone in a bad mood! Everything seems to be dry and cracked and, in some places, the bark is even flaking off, revealing the blotchy, rough skin underneath. Little roots are dangling helplessly in midair, and look like hard, scratchy stubble. Winter's ears and nose are broken branches, and above the dark, shaded eyes a little arching root forms a clumsy eyebrow. The swollen mouth, which is made from a sponge, looks sad, and this toothless old fellow with his thin head of hair gazes longingly into the distance. The only vibrant colors are given off by the lemon and the orange—fruits from the warm south for the north during the cold winter. The old man has no coat to keep him warm and is wrapped only in a thin straw mat. Look more closely and perhaps you can just make out the coat of arms on it with two crossed swords. What kind of symbol is this, do you think? It is actually a reference to the family of the person who originally asked for this picture to be painted.

These strange figures do not only represent the four seasons, but also four different ages and temperaments: youthful Spring is cheerful, mature Summer smiles happily, aging Autumn seems to be enjoying himself, and gloomy Winter is a crusty, old man.

But why did the artist paint such peculiar pictures? Who did he paint these pictures for? And who exactly was Giuseppe Arcimboldo anyway? One thing is certain: he was a master of his art— a magician with a paintbrush!

Arcimboldo, Arcimboldi, Arcimboldus

Giuseppe Arcimboldo was the name of the magical painter, who must have been a very self-willed individual, for he signed his name three different ways: sometimes as Arcimboldo, other times as Arcimboldi or even Arcimboldus. He also wrote his first name in different ways: sometimes as Giuseppe, other times as Josephus or Joseph, spelling his name according to his mood. The path he followed in life and in his artistic career was also an unusual one, which took him far away from his home—which was Milan, Italy, where he was born in 1527—to the royal courts of Vienna and Prague.

Join in the celebrations!

Emperor Ferdinand I, who got to know Archimboldo and began to value his work on one of his many trips through Italy, wanted nothing more than to have him join his Court in Vienna. An intellect as noble and ingenious as this painter's was very highly valued, and Arcimboldo was not only to become Court Portrait Painter, but, in the course of the many years he spent there, he was to become responsible for organizing countless festivities and for overseeing royal outings— something that today would be called "public relations." Although the members of the imperial Habsburg family were perpetual pleasure-seekers, the extravagant celebrations also fulfilled a political function. With its capital in Vienna, and later in Prague, the enormous empire had to be held together somehow—something that was not always easy, for wars broke out regularly. So, as festivities and tournaments made life more exciting and helped people forget the intrigues and danger of everyday life, the aristocracy loved to celebrate as often as possible.

Painter of Kings and Emperors

Giuseppe Arcimoldo entered the employment of Vienna's Imperial Court in the year 1562. He probably never dreamed that he would stay there as long as he did. For twenty-five years— no less than a quarter of a century—he lived and worked at Court, serving as an artist to three generations of emperors and kings.

He maintained very close relationships with his royal patrons. Emperor Maximilian II and Arcimboldo were even the same age. Under this sovereign's patronage, he painted the four seasons (see pages 2-9) and the elements (see pages 20-27), which made him very famous. In 1583, Arcimboldo accompanied the new emperor to Prague. His name was Rudolf II, and it was he who raised Arcimboldo and his family to the aristocracy. At this time, a painter would never have dreamed of being paid a higher honor than this.

By the time he returned home in 1587, a rich and eventful life lay behind him at the Habsburg Court. And, because Rudolf II was so sad when Arcimboldo left Prague, the artist painted an extraordinary portrait of the emperor as Vertumnus, the God of gardens and the changing seasons (see pages 18–19). But that's another story . . .

The magician-painter, Giuseppe Arcimboldo, died on July 11, 1593. Although once highly respected and very famous, he was soon forgotten. But in this book we can rediscover his fascinating pictures which draw us into an enthralling world of magic.

A topsy-turvy world!

¡pluoʍ ʎʌɹnʇ-ʎsdoʇ A

Here Arcimboldo shows us a big, fat onion and some carrots neatly lined up in a row. It's seems to be an ordinary bowlful of vegetables, although somehow there is something peculiar about them . . . And why do you think this painting is called "The Vegetable Gardener"?

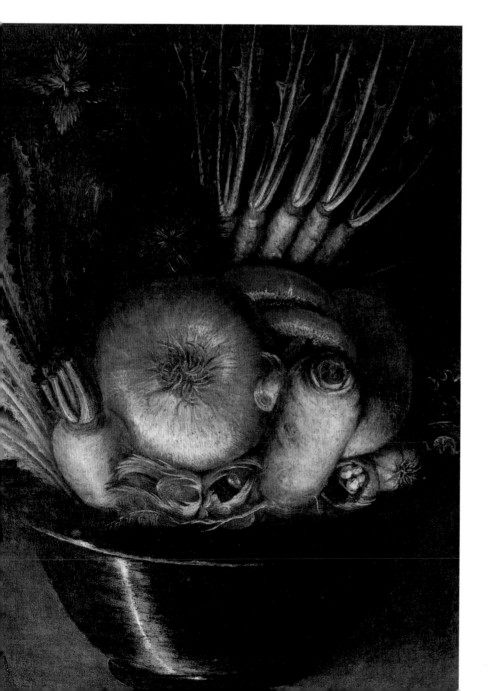

The vegetable gardener is upside-down— or is it the bowl? You can turn it as you like—there are two pictures in one! What a strange way to paint!

This style of painting was known as Mannerism, and was common in this period, when artists wished to break all the rules that had been established by past generations. Arcimboldo certainly painted his bowl of vegetables in this spirit, as you can see.

Turn it upside-down and have a look!
¡ʞool ɐ ǝʌɐɥ puɐ uʍop-ǝpᴉsdn ʇᴉ uɹnꞱ

Let's peek behind the scenes . . .

Life at the Habsburg Court must have been colorful and exciting. Artists and scientists of all nationalities continually came and went, and each day was filled with a mixture of scientific innovation and lively festivities. Emperor Maximilian II loved plants of all kinds and had some of the finest specimens sent to him from all corners of the earth. But he was also keenly interested in books and even had his own librarian, Wolfgang Lazius, whose sole responsibility it was to take care of the emperor's ever-expanding collection.

In his pictures, Giuseppe Arcimboldo depicted different aspects of life at court in his own peculiar way.

Who is this bookworm?

Two books on the left, two books on the right.
And a propped-up volume serves as his cheek.
But be careful! Don't touch them,
Or else the 'book man' will collapse.
Is he more book or more man?
In any case, he's made entirely from books,
As he looks at us earnestly through his dark glasses.
No doubt he's a real bookworm, isn't he!
Who do we really see here, do you think?

It is, in fact, the emperor's librarian, Wolfgang Lazius.

He must have had fun!

This lawyer doesn't look very friendly, does he?

In fact, he's quite horrible!

Look at his face—it's half meat and half fish.

A plucked bird lends him his listless eye,

Which echoes the shape of his stern eyebrows

And his large, gnarled nose,

With a slimy fish as his gaping mouth.

Scholarly books and papers make up his paunch,

After all, law is his profession.

Who do we see here, do you think?

Most likely it is the lawyer Dr. Zasius.

Merriment or mockery? Arcimboldo showed

no mercy to Dr. Zasius, who was one of the Emperor's close advisors. The hard-working lawyer seems to be very cross and his features are all contorted. He looks like a first-rate cheat! Lazius the librarian seems much friendlier, though he is not a bookworm of real flesh and blood. Was the painter perhaps poking fun at these men and their professions? At the time he painted these pictures, anyone would have recognized these men immediately. Courtiers would have been very amused: "What? A man made from a fish and a bird whose feathers have been plucked? A man of books? That's absurd!" Instead of laughing, however, most people probably stood in awe of the paintings and marveled at the artist's skill, for in one thing there can be no doubt: Arcimboldo had fun with the most masterly of means.

Hello, Fruit Face! The emperor
who wished he had been an artist . . .

In 1576, Rudolf II succeeded his father Maximilian II to the throne.
In 1583, he sought the quiet life by moving into his rambling palace,
Hradčany Castle in Prague. There, he was able to dedicate himself to
his life's passions: art and science. He amassed unusual rocks, precious
paintings, sculptures and exotic animals for his cabinet of curiosities and
art collections. Rudolf was painfully shy and slightly eccentric, but he was
also a very clever ruler who understood something about art. With great
enthusiasm, he received the painting that Arcimboldo sent him from
Milan—the picture of himself as Vertumnus, the God of gardens and
the changing seasons.

Rudolf II loved his friend's funny portrait!

The fruit-faced emperor was a famous ruler.
With a blackberry and a cherry for eyes and round apples
for cheeks, he continues to look at us today with his kind smile.
The pear nose is right in the middle of his face. Fruit, vegetables
and flowers from all seasons are depicted in this picture.
The emperor is crowned with grapes and fruit, which are
decorated with flowers and vines. A pumpkin forms the center
of his proudly swollen chest. What a magnificent figure!
This portrait includes many things that we've already seen
in the pictures of the four seasons. Do you recognize Spring's
dress, the fruits of Summer and Autumn's crown of grapes?
But there is much more here. In front of us, we can see
Emperor Rudolf II as a king of fruit and vegetables, and yet
he somehow resembles a god. He is, after all, pictured here
as Vertumnus. He is watching wisely over Nature and
the changing seasons, just as Rudolf kept a vigilant eye on
the fate of his empire. Giuseppe Arcimboldo had so much
fun painting this wonderful and unusual picture that
the emperor could do little more than join in with him!

What things go to make up our world?

There are the four elements:
the earth that we tread on,
the water that we drink,
the air that we breathe,
and fire that keeps us warm.

But, of course, there are also
the animals that run and jump on the earth,
the fish that swim and splash in the water,
the birds that fly and soar through the air,
and wood that crackles and pops in the fire.

All the animals on the earth . . .

All the animals in this picture live together peacefully:
an ox, a donkey, an elephant, stags, a fox, a hare,
a lion, a ram, a horse, a monkey and many, many more.
But, as you can see, together they form a human face!

Where are the eyes, the nose and the mouth of this gentleman?
When seen from a distance they become easier to make out.

The open mouth of a fox is an eye, while its rounded back is a cheek.
A hare forms the bulbous nose, and a wild cat's head is the upper lip.
The tip of the elephant's trunk forms the lower lip,
while the elephant's ear is also a human one.
Several stags, an ibex, a mountain goat, a monkey, a horse
and many other animals combine to make up the hair.
The lion's mane and the ram become the clothing,
while the ox is the collar.

Voilà! A man emerges before our very eyes!

Which sea creatures can you see here?

A ray, a sunfish, an octopus, a seal,
a seahorse, a starfish, a walrus,
a shrimp, a mussel, a crab, a turtle,
and a rock lobster . . .

All the creatures in the water . . .

This mixed-up marine muddle shows us Water's face! Of course! You can easily see the big eye of the sunfish as the lady's eye. This slippery figure is richly adorned with a pearl necklace and pearl earrings. A crab, a turtle and a lobster form the upper part of her body. A ray clings to her shellfish shoulder, while an eel wraps itself around her neck like a piece of fine jewelry. Her cheek is a ray, and beneath that there is a fierce shark showing off its fearsome set of teeth. With an expression of surprise, a moray eel peers out like a nose behind the sunfish. Above the eye a shrimp reclines comfortably, forming an eyebrow. The ear-shaped shell is easy to spot. A seahorse flutters next to it, leading us to the sprightly school of fish that forms the hair. The coral curls on his forehead are funny looking, or is this a very stylish crown? The spikes next to it almost resemble a little coronet.

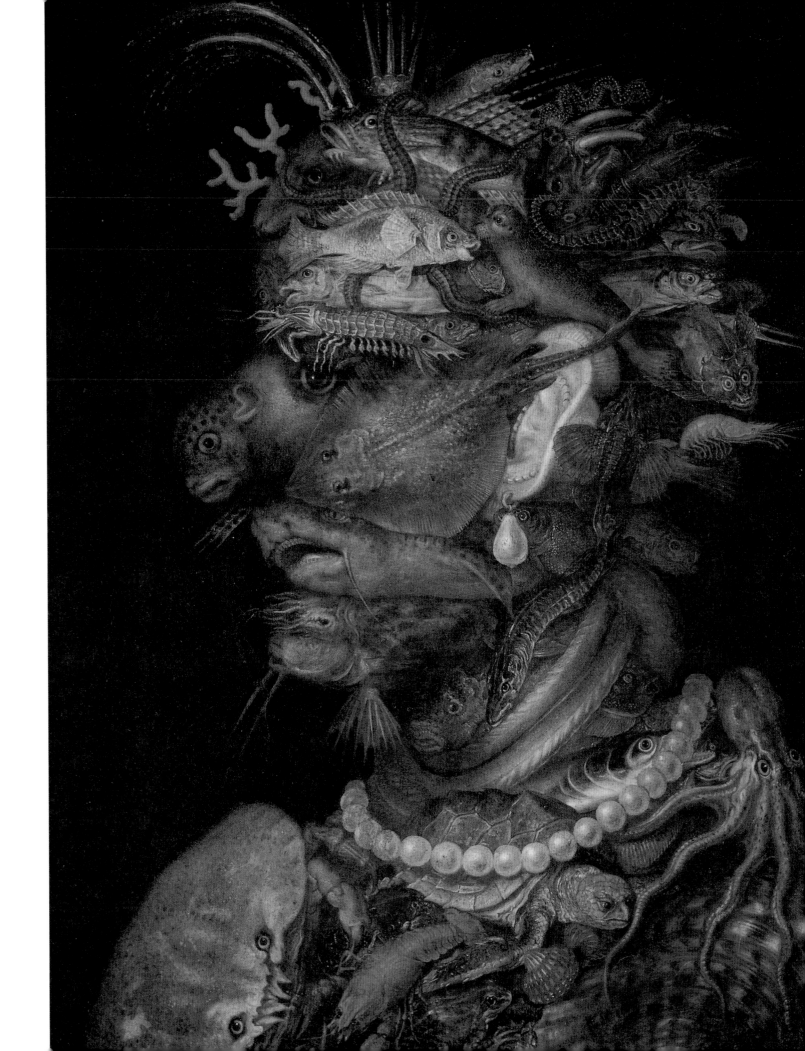

A flock of feathered friends!

Here we have a motley crew:
a peacock and a parrot,
an ostrich and an owl,
a pheasant and a hen,
and lots and lots of ducks!
Together, they form a head seen from the side.
I wonder what he's looking at, don't you?

All the birds in the air . . .

Fat and stout, the turkey has planted himself right in the middle!
His head and chest form a red nose,
while the duck's quacking bill is the slit of an eye.
A goose is sitting in the place of an ear, next to the head of a hen,
and those of two other chickens, making a gaping mouth.
The pheasant's long tail feather shoots out from underneath
like a human chin with a stylishly pointed beard.
The ostrich's long neck is also the man's neck.
The peacock proudly displays its fine feathers.

What a splendid robe he is wearing!

How did people light a fire in days of old?

They used a flint and steel just like the ones which form the cheek, nose and ear of this "hot-head." But, he is also made up of many other "firey" instruments. The burning candle has set the head of red, shaggy hair in flames. Beneath the mustache of wooden matchsticks, an oil lamp can be seen. But be careful! This man is highly explosive! He burns, he blazes, he crackles and smokes. You can warm yourself up just by looking at him! The cannons at the bottom of the picture don't look any less menacing. From the magnificent necklace, a double-headed eagle can be seen next to the head of a ram, the so-called Golden Fleece—a symbol of the highest order: this is the coat of arms of the Habsburgs.

So these four pictures now fall into place. Arcimboldo painted all four elements to honor the Habsburg family.

Long live the Habsburgs!

Arcimboldo wanted to celebrate the Habsburg dynasty with these four pictures of the elements, as though the family's power were as immortal as earth, water, air, and fire . . . and as peace-loving as the animals depicted in his paintings. It is only Fire who appears to have somewhat more spirit, which is fitting since he represents the military strength of the imperial family.

The world, however, is not made up only of the four elements, but also includes the four seasons. With his pictures of the seasons, Arcimboldo aimed to show how the power of the emperors had been as natural and as divinely inspired as spring, summer, autumn and winter. And, just as the seasons can be relied upon to return year after year, the Habsburgs were to continue ruling their empire with a firm but steady hand for many, many years.

What do you think would happen if the pictures could talk to each other
and each element found its matching season?

Now we can see who they are looking at.

Air and Spring

Perhaps they are amusing themselves ...

Summer and Fire

... by telling stories about the long and
peaceful reign of the imperial family.

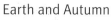
Earth and Autumn

They are probably also talking to each other about
the Italian painter **Giuseppe Arcimboldo**,
who, on his canvases, magically breathed life into
an entirely new world of painting.

Winter and Water

28